Gamechanger

Maximize Your Potential for Success

Rudy Treminio

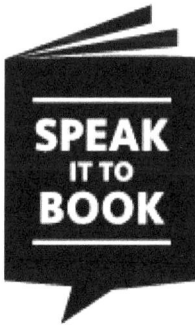

SPEAK IT TO BOOK

Copyright © 2019 by **Rudy Treminio**

Speak It To Book
www.speakittobook.com

Gamechanger / Rudy Treminio
ISBN-13: 978-1-945793-97-4

To my wife and kids—
I've always loved you, and I always will

CONTENTS

My Success Is Your Success

I know what it's like to struggle.

I've been in the place where I can't pay rent. The place where I don't know what, or if, I'll eat next. Questions like how I'm going to manage a good attitude at work when work doesn't pay enough to make ends meet.

I know the fear, the hopelessness, the feeling that life is pointless because I can't pay bills, can't feed myself, can't be a productive member of society.

You might have the same troubles. Take a moment and breathe. Know that it will be okay.

I know you'll be okay because I was there. They said I wouldn't make it because I had nothing. I wouldn't amount to anything because I was too cocky, too uneducated. No one could help. My parents had given up everything just to get us to the United States from El Salvador. And over the course of my life, I took the nothing I was handed and made myself into a gamechanger.

No matter where you are in life, you can be a gamechanger by stepping up your game—by bringing your best. Those are easy words to say, but it's not always easy to do. That's where I come in. I want to share the secrets to success I've found along my way from having nothing to being a winner.

As I drive toward greater success, I want those around me to have a space where they can achieve the greatness I've found. I'm not bragging—I'm just saying it how it is. No one gave me the opportunity for success, so I had to take it. Now that I have my business, I create opportunities for people. That's why I've written this book. You don't have to make the same mistakes I made or waste hours searching for ways to be a gamechanger, because it's inside this book.

I want to make it. I want you to make it. I want to help you because if I help you, I'm not just helping you: I'm helping your spouse, your kids, the people around you. And then you give opportunities to others, and the ripples spread like waves on water. Soon, we're all finding success. We're all making it—together.

Sales can be one of the most rewarding lines of work, both monetarily and in the satisfaction of connecting the right goods to the right people. It's about making people happy. There's no reason to hold back. Learn what you can about sales from those who have found success, and go all in!

You can be a gamechanger, like me. Read on to learn how my story unfolded and what it means for your life and your career. At the end of each chapter, workbook sections will help you become a gamechanger in your own life. We can do this together!

CHAPTER ONE

Be a Gamechanger

I think outside of the box. Why? You must think differently than others if you want to be unique in this world and in the business of sales. To be a gamechanger, you have to be different. If you want to be outstanding, you have to be standing out.

For example, I tried something new in the automotive industry. I asked for funding to plaster my face on the dealer's website and on billboards. The move was risky. Everyone as a general manager tried other things, such as putting up pictures of cars or featuring great deals. However, I thought outside the box and rebranded the dealership. I believed if I built up my name with customers, they would want to buy a Rudy Treminio car—to purchase a car from El Patronn. The dealer agreed.

I disrupted the industry. Suddenly, someone (I) was trying something new. Other businesses took notice that customers were pausing and saying, "Hey, I saw him on YouTube and Facebook. He's famous." All that energy I was putting out came back to me. I gave my best, focusing on the positive, and it all returned tenfold.

As I moved forward with the plan, I set the following priorities:

- Be confident. I knew I would be a game-changer. This meant I could not show doubt. I had to be confident.

- Be positive. It's easy to fall in the trap of being negative. Negativity is picked up by the customer, giving them bad vibes.

- Be proactive. I wanted to be different, so I threw myself fearlessly into social media. People thought I was crazy, but I moved ahead and created a huge following.

What do you notice about each of the previous points? Each involves emotion. Doubt, negativity, and fear have no place in the life of a gamechanger. Yes, you'll feel them, but you learn to set them aside as you push forward.

How do you set aside the fear of being a gamechanger?

The gamechanger is ahead of everyone else—alone, but confident. Yet confidence is the hardest thing to feel. How can you stay poised when you're simply trying to figure it all out? You generate content like crazy, grabbing hold of any idea that has potential so you can capitalize on all of that productivity, but you're still not sure whether it's going to work.

The secret is passion. You must have passion—passion to drive and sell, to go beyond yourself to do what many believe is impossible. Passion pushes out doubt, negativity, and fear.

So many people are washed out in marketing because they lack the passion to rise above. Without passion, they can't work past burnout, failures, and setbacks. Passion to be a gamechanger pushes you to see failures as chances to learn, low sales numbers as opportunities, and detractors as motivation.

I put these thoughts to the test, and businesses took

note. My goal was to brand the dealership at a local level, but now it's known internationally. Now I have owners calling me saying, "This guy is a visionary. He is changing the game." I am putting content out there and being successful. They want my energy.

Sometimes they try to be seen with me for status. They want to say they know me. One person told me, "I have been watching you for a year, and you are the most amazing guy in the car business."

The company didn't give me orders to be a gamechanger. I took the initiative to open up channels for myself. On the side, I became a CEO of an app, and I am pushing the app everywhere. Now I know the app world.

Do you see what's happening here? My passion is focused, and people are doing the word-of-mouth work for me. All I'm doing is marketing, promoting self, and the sales happen. And like with the app, I expand my knowledge as much as possible.

Stand Above the Rest

I think differently than most people. I am a disruptor. I don't like cookie-cutter lives, marketing, or products. I am a custom kind of guy. People prefer custom things, like custom cars, because they're unique.

A gamechanger is someone who doesn't go with the flow, but instead wants to make a unique difference— changing the game not just for him, but for the world. And the passion is so strong, gamechangers don't let discouragement stop their efforts. Acting like others is what makes me frustrated. I'm not like the industry, so I don't want to act that way.

To stand out, I customize the way the industry tells me how to do things. You can do this as well. Don't go by industry standards. For example, customize social media to work for you, and help others customize as well. I promote my team at the dealership personally because their faces are just as important as mine.

My customers have a different experience because they are used to going back and forth over the price of the car. In other dealerships, customers ask if this price will work, and the salesperson will disappear and usually come with a different number. The customer will request another price, and the cycle will start again. Instead of haggling, I take them to the office with a business manager and a sales manager and figure out the best price for the customer. They are like, "Huh, that's different." They don't do that at the other dealerships. For us, though, it's about finding a win-win experience for both our customer and our business.

Most people are content with the status quo and just go with the flow, existing merely to do the mundane things day after day. But the status quo is boring at best and a death for your business at worst. I don't go with the flow. I do the opposite. Even when the economy is in a bad stretch, and businesses are hunkering down to weather a bad month, I say, "No—we are going to find a way to figure it out. We'll change things up and make sales grow."

Be Yourself

You have to be what you believe in. If you're not, customers know. And the feeling that something isn't quite right is a death ring to a sale.

This is where passion is important. When you are yourself, you're going to come against people unhappy that their lives are disrupted because you're beating their sales numbers. Or you're changing up the office and making him or her look bad. When you go opposite of everyone else, you stand out, and many see this as bad. You must be aware that some people are going to be uncomfortable that you are disrupting the workplace, and the market.

Be who you are meant to be. Be passionate about it. You have to share with the world. There isn't a lot of people doing good in business because they are scared of who they are. Being who you are means being passionate about saying "I am going to be me. I am going to be who I am and what I believe in."

The road of sales takes a particular path. Most people don't have good processes that fit themselves. I have procedures that have been proven good in the car business and take me to the next level. Be who you are means your identity that's unique from everyone else. However, for the competition, customers will expect a higher standard, so things are starting to change for them, so some see it as a threat.

Some are scared of people who are themselves. Some people can't stand it. Disrupting the industry and the ending cookie-cutter system must be stopped. Personally, I don't like anything to do with cookie-cutter, and I love customization. The public wants a different show. They are tired of the status quo. Tired of the routine. When I share what I feel and what I am passionate about, when I am raw and real, I connect with the customer. I am going to be who I am. Some people don't like authentic people.

You create that audience because you are real. I can be the same way all the time because people relate to me. They aren't showing that fake side of themselves because of fear of rejection, because I'm open about how much I like them. I'm not afraid that I'm an open book. I share myself with the world. I share my bad and good.

Some people in sales aren't ready for authenticity. It's weird to them, or they are scared. They just don't want to put themselves out there that way.

Bottom line? My sales are better because of my authenticity, and I'm successful.

Everyone needs to be themselves. So, what's the process? How do you become authentic in sales, filled with passion so that you can be a gamechanger?

I wasn't born this way. I needed to grow into who I am. Here's my story—and how it can help you.

WORKBOOK

Chapter One Questions

Question: What are you passionate about? If you feel little to no passion for your career, what needs to change—your line of work, your workplace, or your attitude/approach? IIow does a lack of passion lead to a lack of confidence, as well as negativity and mediocrity?

_____

_____

_____

_____

_____

_____

_____

_____

_____

_____

Question: Are you authentic with your customers/clients and coworkers? Are you known for your honesty and genuineness or do you spout off rehearsed lines and manifest artificial concern? What are some ways that you can make real and ongoing connections with your team and with the people you are trying to reach with your business?

_____

_____

_____

_____

_____

_____

_____

_____

_____

_____

_____

Action: Make a list of five ideas that would position you to be a gamechanger. You need ideas that are unique, creative, customized—and possibly risky. Research your ideas to see what is needed to carry out each one. Then choose one to begin implementing this week.

_____

_____

_____

_____

_____

_____

_____

_____

_____

_____

_____

_____

Chapter One Notes

_____

_____

_____

_____

_____

_____

_____

_____

_____

_____

_____

_____

_____

_____

_____

_____

_____

_____

_____

_____

_____

CHAPTER TWO

Finding the Drive to Succeed

El Salvador is a poor country. Finding food takes up the majority of your time, and most days, you go to bed starving.

The surest way for a young man to find enough to eat is to join a gang. Sure, you have to do what they tell you and make money by selling drugs, stealing, and an occasional killing, but if you don't join, you're dead. And your family probably is, as well. There are different gangs everywhere, and territory wars are constant. You live in a fear because they have no respect for life.

Nothing changes. The poverty, the filth, the suffering. There's no growth, no way to get out of it. You simply try to survive, day after day, and with a salary of $200 a month, you can't subsist.

There is no future. How can a person start a family? There is no water and no toilets and there are animals running all around. In some areas today, there are more modernized homes. But mostly, people craft a house wherever and with whatever they can find.

Falling in love still happens. Couples want to come together, have children. But in this environment? But there is a dream—a dream to come to the United States. A dream where you can work hard and give those you love a better life. If you own a business in the United States, no matter how small, you have more power than the authorities in El Salvador.

My childhood in El Salvador was dark and focused on survival.

How I Survived

My mother left when I was six. Between the ages of six through ten, I was involved with the wrong crowd. My grandmother was older, and she couldn't control me. One could say I was the black sheep. I was running around doing what I wanted to. I didn't pay attention to what little education that was offered. Instead, I went to school just to be part of the crowd. No one paid attention to me. My uncle was working. My aunt lived in the city. And my grandmother was too feeble to keep up with a wild child. I never graduated from high school.

And then, against my will, at age fifteen, I was shuttled off to the United States to be with my parents.

Yes, against my will. Why? Why, when the American dream was supposed to be what everyone wanted? I had the chance to be whatever I wanted, and yet I didn't want to leave my sorry existence?

Because I wasn't supposed to be successful. I didn't have an education. I was supposed to be like everyone else who emigrated from another country—an underpaid laborer never rising to more. And even though the American lifestyle was considered better, safer, more upscale—I didn't like the change. I didn't like the new way. Fifteen years in one culture, and I was hit with culture shock coming to a new place.

It's funny, I hated driving everywhere. Of all the things you have to adjust to, I couldn't get over the fact I couldn't just walk where I wanted to go. Distances were too far.

My mind was always drifting back to my home in El Salvador. It proved impossible to break this habit. I overcame, and continue to overcome, the language, culture, and food, because you have to get used to it. But bottom line, I didn't like being here.

Then, something in my head clicked. If I had to be here, what could I do to make the best of it. And more importantly, what advantages did I have that others didn't have?

Everyone Is Against Me

The idea that everyone was against me took hold. No matter where I was, El Salvador or the United States, I didn't have the history and education to be successful. I was an out-of-shape punk who was so complacent I'd rather be in a tough environment where all I had to do was be part of a gang instead of working to make something of myself. In both places, I wasn't going to amount to much. Was it my fault I was dealt these cards?

I liked the idea that everything was against me. I wasn't supposed to be successful. I didn't speak English. The adversity of my position showed plainly on my features, advertising me as the failure I was, so no one was going to take a chance on me. I had to adjust to a baffling culture where people went on diets because there was so much food. And I had no idea how to take advantage of opportunities.

Assets Instead of Disadvantages

I was miserable and knew I needed to change not only myself, but also my circumstances. I began to think about what I had that others didn't have. As I thought about it, and looked at other Americans, I realized I had many advantages. One important distinction struck me: I was *thinking* about my advantages. Others didn't think about what they had but others didn't have. Just the thought experiment alone was an advantage, setting me apart from others.

Once I realized I was unique in one little way, advantages started coming to mind.

Languages. I was fluent in Spanish, and I realized, if I wanted new friends, I would have to perfect my English. Both languages could be a huge asset.

Two markets. With two languages, I could sell things for the Spanish market and the English market. People like dealing with others from their own area that speak their own language. They relate to you. They feel like you are helping them in a way. And with English, it meant I could communicate with any American. What could I do, though?

Sales. I'd always sold myself to people. I want friends, so I brought forward my best traits. What if I brought forward the great things in a product that people need? It just felt natural. I would sell. And I could do it in both English and Spanish markets.

Different languages. Not only was speaking languages important, as I tried to fit in, I learned I could speak to people at a different level than, *"Hola, ¿cómo estás?"* Language was about finding out where people are, what they need, and how I can help. That means relating with them and cultivating friendships.

I discovered every person has advantages over other people. It's not a competition. When we come together to use our assets, combining our forces for a single cause, it's a great opportunity for all.

But these were just thoughts, swirling around in my head. They were there, but I had no idea what to do with them. What's more, I didn't even know if I wanted to do anything with them. My complacency was acting like a choke collar and something had to break. I struggled against a system of education and language that threatened to strangle the life out of me. The culture was new, the people were strange, and the pressure to be someone was killing me.

That's when I made the biggest decision of my life.

WORKBOOK

Chapter Two Questions

Question: What is your story? How have you gotten to where you are in your career—is it the path you always planned to take, or did you end up here through a lot of twists and turns?

_____

_____

_____

_____

_____

_____

_____

_____

_____

_____

Question: When Rudy changed his perspective, he went from complacency to confidence. What are some areas in your life where you have settled for complacency or mediocrity? How are you selling yourself short? What could your life be like if you changed your perspective? Who could help you in changing your perspective to one that is healthy and proactive?

_____

_____

_____

_____

_____

_____

_____

_____

_____

_____

_____

Action: List out the things that you tend to see as disadvantages in your background. How can each these become an asset in effectively reaching people and having the confidence and creativity to become a gamechanger?

_____

_____

_____

Chapter Two Notes

CHAPTER THREE

Success Starts with You

Being a teen is difficult enough when handling a changing body and emotions, trying to fit in, wondering what the future holds, and figuring out what part you have to play in this world. All the while, you're trying to find freedom and fun, which sets you against the discipline of parents and teachers. My situation was complicated by the move from El Salvador to the United States.

So, I moved out of my parent's house. Here's what happened.

A Loner

In El Salvador, I had friends and a group that I hung with. We found plenty of trouble. My childhood was fun from my perspective. I was considered the black sheep of the family, and I didn't really care.

Then I was moved to the United States. I hated the food, and the environment was stiff and controlled. There were people from so many countries, such variety of people and lifestyles, and I was used to El Salvador where everyone wore the same hairstyle, the same clothes, lived the same expectations, and frankly, life moved slower—

which made me complacent.

Instead of diving into the new cultures and opportunities, I rebelled. I pushed everyone and everything away. I didn't do anything bad, and I didn't hang out with the wrong people. Instead, I did nothing at all and didn't hang out with anyone. I didn't make changes and didn't start over like I should have done. I let culture shock win.

School was extremely difficult. Language was a barrier I couldn't overcome. I love talking with people and found my lack of English restricting. Secondly, U.S. social and legal constraints restricted the kind of freedom I had enjoyed in El Salvador. With all the rules laid down, I couldn't do what I wanted—and what's worse, keeping track of all the rules and laws proved to be more than I could handle. I couldn't figure out what was going on.

From a popular bad-boy and a jock, I quickly became a stress-eating fat-guy loner. People talked about me a lot. I didn't understand the language, but I knew. Sneers and bullying translate into any language.

At this low point, I decided to find love.

Finding Love

After high school, I left home. At eighteen, I was going to be a father. The mother wasn't from the same culture, and when she and I left the house to get married, no one came. We were alone. There was no celebration, no congratulations—we were just married.

Living outside of my parents' house meant I needed work. While I had a few loose principles to help me proceed, I struggled. By the time my son was born, we were back home in my parent's basement.

Learning Skills

I had no choice. I had to get work that paid enough to

house and care for a family. Delivering pizza wasn't going to work.

Deep inside, I knew I was meant for more. I could be more, do more, and be happy. As I thought more on my skillsets and advantages that might put me in front of others, my heart settled on car sales. Not only could I make something of myself, I could bring in serious money for my burgeoning family.

But before I could get started, I needed to learn how to sell.

I walked into a dealer and asked the manager, "Can I have a job?"

"What experience do you have?"

With those five words, I was shot down. It's the biggest catch-22 in business: Where am I going to get experience if everyone only hires people with experience?

But a starving baby and an unhappy wife propelled me on. I tried somewhere else, looking for someone who would let me sell cars. Someone said yes, but first, he wanted me to start out as a car jockey—detailing and cleaning cars.

I knew that I wanted to do sales.

I knew I had sales in me. With my Spanish, I would have been better than most of them, since most didn't speak Spanish despite the many Spanish-speaking customers.

I didn't give up. I went to two different managers, and they asked why I traveled two hours to be there. They wanted to see how badly I wanted it. I kept coming back. I found a persistency in me and I knew I was not going to give up. I wanted to do it. I wanted to be successful.

I went to a dealership my friend worked at, and the manager asked me, "Why do you want to do this?" I knew from my friend this dealership was popular with great sales numbers. One aspect that made me want this job was they did sales training on Fridays.

I replied, "I want an opportunity. I want you to give me a shot. I want to learn this." I really wanted the extra training, so I added, "I will buy the shirts, don't worry about that. I will wear a tie. I will buy whatever I need."

He looked at me for a moment, and finally said, "Come to my training session on Friday."

That was the car dealership where I started. They would train us for different scenarios. I shadowed my friend for a little while to learn his style, and then I gave it my own twist. I learned how to close the deal.

Lessons Learned

What sale would you turn down? If they have the money, want the goods, what would make you say no? Of course you're going to close the sale.

I told people no even before I tried to sell something to them. I judged people. Everyone does.

Don't judge a person by their cover. You never know what the person is going to do. It's like telling them no, they can't buy the car.

One day, a person who looked like a bum bought five cars from me. Five.

He wore a ripped shirt and a tank top, shorts, and flip flops. The guy didn't look like he had a penny to his name. All the salespeople prejudged him. Since I was a low man, I listened to what he was interested in, grudgingly showed him around, and then things got serious. When I closed on the five cars, I felt like a new man. Not only did I feel like sales was for me, I would never prejudge a customer for what they looked like.

Sometimes the customer that you think is not going to work is a great sale, and those who look like big money spenders hold back and fight for impossible deals. It doesn't matter. You have to do your job one hundred percent.

This attitude took me places.

I started doing the small but powerful things that make car salesmen great.

I learned:

- Follow up on referrals.

- Make the customer comfortable enough they didn't need to negotiate the price.

- All dealers have similar cars, even the same brand and year of vehicles, but the experience is what people desire the most. If you give them a different experience than everyone else that's going to separate you to the top.

- If you treat customers like human beings and not like numbers, you will go further.

- I've noticed that most customers shop around seven dealerships but makes a decision based on two dealerships. Outshine the other one.

- Prices are important, but not how you think. People nowadays are willing to pay higher for better service.

But I also learned lessons from my own tendencies. I'm a perfect example of a guy who will just order a product online. Sometimes I'll pay more on the shipping than the cost of the item because of the ease of online shopping. What does that mean? It means I'm not in the mood to deal with a salesperson. As a salesman, I learned to always emphasize on the experience.

If you give them a wow factor, you will leave them with memories they are going to remember long after the car is gone. You interact with them. They are already coming to the dealership with their fists out, ready to fight for what they want or to haggle a price. They already come with the feeling that you are a crook, that your job is to take their money.

How do you give them the wow factor?

- Learn their name.

- Care. Honestly care. This matters to them, and it should matter to you.

- Help them with their finances. If they know you're looking after their wallet, then they know you're on their side.

- Don't look at them just as a sale. They're not. It's about educating them. And connecting the right goods to fit their needs.

- Stop selling so much. Stop being so pushy. Everyone wants to buy a car.

- It's rare that people don't care about service and just want the rock bottom deal. Most people want to be treated like humans. Learn the difference in their manner.

When you give the experience, that wow factor, to the customer, they notice because you leave an impression to them. You can't have a second impression, but there is always a first impression.

Starting out, I was inspired by the men and women at the top. If there are people in charge who treat the customer right, it spreads through the sales team. If the top is just interested in money, and they are greedy, the salesmen will be the same.

I saw one salesman got a repeat customer, and I asked him how he managed to get them to come back and buy another car from him. He didn't know. So, I studied his style. I noticed that after he finished the sale, he treated them like heroes and royalty *after* they bought the car. He was thinking long-term and not just about the quick buck.

If you build the relationship and care for them, go out of your way when they call to make sure they have your information and how they can get ahold of you, they will be loyal to you forever.

Today, I still have customers from the Bronx following me wherever I go. I haven't changed my number in over ten years. I don't want to lose my number because most of my clients have that number. They still call me: "Where you at now? My daughter needs a car." Why? Because the experience is so much more important than the price.

I took these lessons and found a permanent home in sales. However, I was far from being a gamechanger. I was about to face one of the most difficult times anyone could ever live through. What I went through, and what I learned, would change me from a moderate salesman to the successful team leader I am today.

WORKBOOK

Chapter Three Questions

Question: What motivates and propels you to work—family, boredom, debt, needs/wants? How bad do you want to succeed, and what are you willing to do to achieve it?

_____

_____

_____

_____

_____

_____

_____

_____

_____

_____

Question: Where do you need more training? Where do you need more experience? What opportunities can you take advantage of to grow in these areas? Where are you giving less than 100 per cent, and how are you missing opportunities because of your attitude?

_____

_____

_____

_____

_____

_____

_____

_____

_____

_____

_____

Action: Look at the bullet list of how to give your customers the "wow" factor. Rate yourself on a scale of 1-10 on how well you are doing in each of these areas. Then ask a coworker and/or a former customer to rate you as well. Find a coworker, mentor, or family member who will role-play with you so that you can practice building relationships and giving a memorable experience.

_____

_____

_____

_____

_____

_____

_____

_____

_____

_____

_____

Chapter Three Notes

_____

_____

_____

_____

_____

_____

_____

_____

_____

_____

_____

_____

_____

_____

_____

_____

_____

_____

_____

_____

CHAPTER FOUR

Adversity and Self-Care

I don't remember leaving the club in the middle of the night.

It was my own fault. I was drunk. Stupid drunk.

At some point, I must have made it to the car. They tell me I was driving across a bridge at 2 a.m. Again, I don't remember.

I awoke on impact.

The airbags popped in my face. Pain shot through my chest. Then, silence. Stunned, it took me an hour to figure out whether I was daydreaming or sleeping. I woke up enough to push open the door and stumble to the street. Another car lay shattered nearby.

Still drunk, I returned to my car and slept until my phone rang. I managed to find it, picked it up, and heard my wife's voice.

Soon, paramedics surrounded the vehicles, pulling us out and checking for injuries. Then the realization hit me: I was going to prison.

How I Got There

There is a strong pull in the car business to work twelve

to eighteen hours a day, grinding, to make a living. The other pull is easier, another path you can take. Quick money. Get money right way. Become popular, become a name through clubbing, drinking, doing drugs, and then you'll sell cars. That was my path.

I was making six figures at age 21. And the lifestyle was appealing. You want to become the lifestyle. You want to be the popular guy. What are in those clubs? People eager to become popular as well, and you are going to become a part of the culture because you are surrounded with similar people. You choose the path you want to take. I chose to be the popular kid. Going to nightclubs and strip clubs.

And yet, the popular lifestyle—the clubbing, and the drinking—hurt the ones I loved most. They would trade the money for a clean, healthy dad. And while I partied, they grew on without me. I figured my family would always be there. I felt as if I gave my life to a job for no reason. Money was just thrown at my family to keep them quiet so I could club.

Then, one night, I was under a lot of pressure and stress. Instead of staying somewhat coherent, I drank to escape and landed in prison. As a consequence, I lost precious time with my kids.

Prison

What was I thinking? My wife was taking care of our kids, and here I was, clubbing to the point I landed in a cell. My face and name were plastered all over the television. Car businesses tuned into the news, and it spread like wildfire. My career and life were over. I really messed up this time.

My bail was $100,000. My parents and wife worked hard to raise the money, and finally put together the bond money. They hired an attorney, and I was let out on bail.

The problem was, I was still working through immigration and would probably get deported.

As I sat in a gray cell on a thin mattress, I looked at my hands. I still had both hands. I stamped my feet on the concrete floor. Both legs worked.

And in that moment, I realized how lucky I had been. I was a complete man, had all of my faculties, and I was locked up by my stupid decisions. Utterly useless. I had it so good, and I threw it all away.

It was a life-changing moment.

Prison was simple survival. Normal people don't belong in prison. The racial divisions divided the population, and everyone was on edge, trying to prove something. If you looked at a guy a certain way, his whole gang was in your face. You quickly learned personalities, along with all the rules and regulations you couldn't break. With the leaders, it was their way or the highway. Fights broke out every five minutes over ridiculous stuff.

When you think of prison, many times you think of a boring time all alone in your cell. I shared the room with sixty-two people, and there was only one bathroom. And people were there for different crimes, all mixed together. There were people who were going away for a long time side by side with others waiting to be sentenced, unsure what was going to happen to them. And for me—one of the worst things ever—I couldn't even have a conversation with people.

However, I knew what was going on outside the walls. They brought in current books and newspapers. It was frustrating to read world events, and yet, what went on outside had nothing to do with the world on the inside. You couldn't act the same way inside as you acted outside. If you broke the code, you got beat up.

I wouldn't back down from a fight. Why? I didn't feel like a criminal. I wasn't one of them. I looked at people who had murdered, raped, robbed, maimed, and knew I shouldn't be there. It was one night, one bad decision, I was just a drunk and I got into an average car accident, caused by my lack of control on one night. But people who look at their cell phones while driving are just as unable to drive.

I started talking with a businessman. He felt the same as me, yet he had a different perspective on the situation: it was only one stupid moment that had caused us to be in this place we shouldn't be, so he was determined to live his life in such a way that he never had to come back.

My mind spun. What did that mean for me?

I had been searching that night—searching for an escape. Life was difficult. I was facing adversity professionally and privately, and I needed a break. Getting drunk was the escape I'd found, but that one moment threatened to ruin my family, career, and any chance I had of success. All because I couldn't face the adversity in my life. My one reckless decision to drive drunk led to repercussions that I'm still dealing with, to this day.

The man I crashed my car into was on the brink of life and death. During my trial, he was in a coma for several months. My lawyer told me that if he died, I would be facing seven to ten years in prison. Thank God, he pulled through, but he's paralyzed. For the rest of his life, he'll never walk again. Every day, I have to deal with knowing how much pain I caused him and will continue to cause him—and I know that my feelings about this completely pale in comparison to whatever he's feeling.

The auto dealership I was working for at the time had to pay out millions of dollars. Afterward, their insurance increased hundreds of thousands of dollars per year, all because of my one horrible, egotistical mistake. The publicity was so bad that they changed their name. There was no way I could work for them again after I got out.

Looking back at my time in prison, I can see that the businessman's simple advice was exactly what I needed to hear. The thought that I was only drinking to escape my problems for a moment made me a better person.

If the hellfire and nightmares I experienced had happened to other people, I can imagine some of them thinking, *"I'm a drunk. Nothing's going to change. I'll always be a dumb boozer."* And that apathy would become their reality.

Not me.

I realized that my addiction had hurt innocent people, and I acknowledged that it would always stop me from succeeding if I let it. But I chose to break the cycle by overcoming my alcoholism.

Many people want to escape from reality, to break away and get so high they don't feel what's going on with the real world, instead of becoming a person who is able to rise above their problems.

Trying to escape instead of overcoming is a mistake that could cost you everything. You don't want to live through those consequences—trust me.

Learning from Mistakes

We're all learning. Here's the problem: success teaches you nothing except that what you did made you popular, rich, and happy. Now, repeat. It's not that easy. There's no repeat. You can't keep doing the same thing over and over to be successful. You have to adapt and expand if you want to be a gamechanger.

After you have success, like I did in the car dealerships, before everything crashed down around me, you've learned one thing that you should do—a narrow thing that works. But when you fail, when something doesn't work, you are able to gather a vast array of data to analyze. You have many paths to avoid.

I learned I couldn't run from my problems. I had to face them. I also learned that all publicity isn't always good publicity. And so much more. Mistakes teach a lesson. Mistakes shape you into who you are because when you are down, when you are at your worst, the bad doesn't need to define you. You can define you if you learn from your mistakes.

Maybe you made a major mistake like I did, ending up in prison. There is a reason why you are going through what you're going through now. It's there for you to learn from. Take advantage and overcome your problem, and you'll be ready to face even more.

Prison was the best thing that happened to me. If I hadn't gotten into that accident, I probably have kept turning to alcohol and eventually died. Perhaps I would have crashed into a pole and not survived. Prison was my wake-up call. As I looked around the cell, I wondered if it was the way I was supposed to live. I asked myself, "Is this who I am now?"

Even though I was learning from my lessons, I didn't want to go home. How was I going to be successful? I was making money, and now, nothing. I was in prison, in over my head, and then my wife visited. She'd been looking to me to change. And when I told her what I was thinking, that I would learn to overcome my problems and never touch alcohol again, she shared what was going on at home.

My kids were doing poorly in school. In fact, their stress was so strong, they needed counseling. Before, they were excelling, but I hadn't seen the blessings I had around me. I took them for granted. That was on me.

Now, they were learning from my mistakes. But my wife and kids stood by me. I couldn't let them go through that again.

Preparing for My Future

I had plenty of time to keep thinking, and my mind

turned to my future and car sales. How was I going to become popular again? So, as my sixteen months in prison were almost up and I prepared for my future, I summed up my thoughts.

- How I earn a living is more important than how much I make—if I earn six figures but lose my family, what's the point of money?

- Success is great but learning from mistakes is better—success offers one lesson, while failure offers many.

- If I can handle adversity, I don't need harmful escapes—and what's more, I can teach others how to work through their adversity.

Handling Adversity

My entire trial came down to my inability to handle adversity. If I were able to manage the trials and troubles of the world, I wouldn't have needed an escape. So, what did I learn about overcoming troubles? Let me break it down for you.

Mindset

I believe in the law of attraction. If you perceive it's the end of the world, then it becomes a self-fulfilling prophecy and you'll make it the end of the world for you. In my mind, I am conscious and aware that no matter how bad something is, I can overcome the issue.

Live a life of forward momentum. When your mind shifts toward problems, pause. Talk to yourself. Words are powerful. Claim truth. Grasp the fact that things aren't the end of the world, and that you will step up to meet this challenge. Say it aloud.

You're not blocking out the problem. Instead, once I step into the mindset of someone who overcomes problems, my mind begins to process how I can handle the issue without hurting other people.

I used to worry about the future. But now, I take it day by day. I do the best I can do in the twenty-four hours I have, because my mindset is that when any problem arises, I'll rise to the challenge and overcome it.

I am a visionary. That means, I dream of the possibilities of the future, then invest time in bettering myself to take care of what's coming. However, I've no idea what the future holds. So with an overcomer mindset, I'm learning as much as I can. Reading, studying, researching—I never know what tip will prepare me to rise higher and leave my legacy.

Mindset is important for those who have a troubled past like mine. Some people get stuck in the past, living there, and get stuck. Change the mindset. The past happened, and there's nothing that can change. Let the past stay where it was—in the past—and learn from it. Then move on.

Here's a list of characteristics of strongminded people:

- They don't hold grudges. Some things do affect or knock a person down for a day or two. But that doesn't define you.

- They know a person's opinion isn't their reality. Shift your state of mind from their words being fact to just listening to their opinion.

- They state the positive. Every time you say something negative, it's the law of attraction, and you are attracting negativity. If you preach positivity to yourself and your belief is positivity, you are going to find other positive things around you.

- They deal with problems and situation that arise. They don't ignore them. They are going to take care of the problem and move ahead, and something positive will come out of it.

- They know the world is going to end. Someday. But today is not that day. So even if they are knocked down, the next day they bounce right back.

Once you have a good mindset, it becomes a habit. My mind just clicks when I see good results, and I want to do it again. Even though there are days I don't want to go to the gym, once I see results, I'm all in. It's automatic. But it starts with a mindset.

Look for *Ah-Ha!* Moments

What's happening to you right now? It's a season, and there's a reason why it happened. Search your memory for the behavior that caused you to get to this place.

Now, the event may be good or bad, but what were your actions that caused you act the way you did? Be honest with yourself, and whatever you do, don't spend all your time finding fault in others. True, they may be at fault. But that was your reaction? How did your respond?

It is reflection process that helps you to grow. Sometimes, once you hit rock bottom, reflecting on events that happened in your life shows the lessons and allows you to move forward. It's the path that you have chosen. Did it spiral out of control? Were you simply trying to maintain a status quo? What are you going to learn from it?

When you see it, it's an *ah-ha!* moment. When I was sitting in prison, I knew I didn't belong there. I thought,

"Why am I going through this right now? Is my Creator trying to tell me something? It's time to learn." Ah-ha!

If you don't learn from your mistake, next time you might be six foot under. It's a reality check. We all watch people who keep making the same mistakes and believe they can't get better, or don't want to, and that's their life. While I needed to go through my trials to understand the right way to live my life, others who undergo painful circumstances and don't learn from them, waste their experience. I had to go through the pain and suffering, through hurting myself, family, and career to get to another level, a level I should have obtained without the pain, but couldn't. It's part of the process. And the process is what you make of it, what you learn from the situation. Something good comes from something bad if you reflect and learn and come to your *ah-ha!* moment.

Now that I had my *ah-ha!* moment, now that I had a positive mindset and a determination to be a new man and handle adversity, what next? How could I reclaim a career? How could I capture a bit of the success I had and do it without hurting my family?

Nothing was going to come easily.

Chapter Four Questions

Question: Do you typically face adversity or run from it? What sort of escape mechanisms do you use? What are some healthy and helpful ways to handle stress and difficulties? What are some practical ways that you can you develop a strong, positive, visionary mindset?

_____

_____

_____

_____

_____

_____

_____

_____

_____

_____

Question: What are some mistakes you have made in your life, and what lessons can you learn from each of them? How can you assimilate those lessons into your life, yet remain future-focused instead of stuck in the past? What *ah-ha!* moments have changed you?

_____

_____

_____

_____

_____

_____

_____

_____

_____

_____

_____

Action: Think about where you want your career to be in five years, ten years, and twenty years. How about your family and friend relationships? Write out a vision statement and put it where you can review it often, especially during seasons of adversity. Make sure that your statement is based on truth and a positive attitude.

_____

_____

_____

Chapter Four Notes

CHAPTER FIVE

Rebuilding

After a sobering experience in prison, I was finally home. I knew immediately I was going to have to rebuild.

I had expected to find a job right away and take off with my new life lessons. I was eager to please my family, bring in a good salary, and find ways to be a gamechanger. In essence, my goal was to return everything to some semblance of normal. I knew I could do it and my family knew I could do it. But I hit a snag.

No one wanted to hire me. I went through over a dozen interviews and over a dozen notifications that led to crushing disappointment. They wouldn't come near me because of my record. Sure, everyone knew I was talented and *the* guy to hire. But because our business is public, the public knew my one mistake, and they labeled me as a felon and an undesirable.

My life was a struggle. I was bummed and started to plummet emotionally. I questioned myself. Did I lose the skills that kept me at the top? Am I valuable to society at all? If I took a different position with less money, would my family make it? Part of me didn't want to give up the high money the sales positions paid, but trying as hard as I could, no car dealership would hire me. People would try to hook me up with jobs that just couldn't match my family's needs. In despair, I went to a small dealership with weak sales and no brand, and I had no say in advertising or promotion. But at least they didn't run a background check.

As I waited for a customer, thinking over the road that led me to this moment, I found I wanted to escape my troubles. The bottle called. With a vengeance. I was desperate to drink away my problems, guzzle into oblivion. And why not? The big dealerships weren't going to take a chance on me.

But I stuck to my convictions. I would not drink. I wouldn't put my family through that again.

The Principles of Rebuilding

Everyone fails. It's how we learn, how we grow. Sometimes, failing means we lose money. Other times, a relationship is hurt. Sometimes a business goes under and we let down our employees and creditors. At other times, we're able to pay off the debts and let the failure become a distant memory.

But my failure had a high cost, and now I was paying it.

The Cost of Family

My wife and I were okay. We talked—a lot. She thought it was funny that I lost weight and worked out in prison, yet I didn't need a trainer to get in shape. It was a physical indication of my mental dedication, that I was more disciplined. But I didn't have money for new clothes, so I just wore my smallest clothes.

What hit hard was the time away from my kids. I was away from the kids for sixteen months, and for a child, that's a lifetime. Prison, behind glass, is not a good place for your kids to see you. You're at your worst. You feel embarrassed. You're the one who let your family down. You are the one who damaged your kids.

And to see me in prison would only make it worse. I didn't want the kids to see me. I was ashamed for my kids to see me that way. So, I asked my wife not to bring them. Though I didn't do much writing, I would call.

When I first talked with them, it was a little awkward. I was away for a really long time. But when I returned home, I had no choice but to spend time with them. The first thing I discovered was that I was a little out of it their routine. I had to get back into their rhythm. I had to get back on the family schedule, not the prison schedule.

What could I do? This is how I handle the transition home:

- I prioritized talking to them.

- Invested in them to show I wanted to rebuild with them.

- Gave them one-hundred percent of my attention when I was with them.

- Taught them life lessons through age appropriate stories of my life.

My kids asked why I had to go away. And I explained that I had not been very responsible, and going away was a consequence. Then, as my relationship with the children grew stronger, my wife trusted me more and the family unity solidified.

Family is always there for you. I will never work on Sundays anymore. I will spend that time and more with family. Before, I worked a lot of hours. I wouldn't see them in the morning or night or barely on Sundays. I would bring work home. When it was time for my family,

I was still mentally at work. But now, I focus on my family. Before it was hard because I wasn't thinking about how my actions affected my family. Sure, I was successful, but not in the ways that truly mattered. Now, even when the busy times come, I always make time for my kids.

The Cost of Reputation

I was a convicted felon. I knew that people would look at me differently. I was on the FBI list for the rest of my life, and there wasn't a thing I could do about it. And what's worse, everyone knew it.

I couldn't do a thing about what people thought of me. You simply can't change their minds once the stigma of felon enters their heads. No matter the crime, no matter the person, it's a label that comes with a heavy price. A price that I had to bear. There was no choice.

So I had to change my lifestyle and mindset. I had to change how I carried myself. In the minds of others, I was criminal or an ex-con. People assumed the worst. People say they aren't prejudice, but then give you a look—one of mistrust and sometimes hatred and disgust. They assume you are a bad person without knowing the details. Regardless of your talents and skillsets, when they see felon on your application, they judge you based on that five-letter word. They didn't care to know what happened or what kind of person I was. They saw ex-con and it was automatically a red flag. I have to live with that label for the rest of my life.

Even though my reputation had holes, I believed something good would come out of the bad. You have to trust the past and work through it. There is a reason you are going through the pain. It could be a lesson or a warning. It depends on how you look at it. Why did that happen? Normally, I avoided driving home drunk. But this one event was meant to teach me something.

Spend time and figure out why you are going through your struggle. What's the root of it? Because knowing yourself, your faults and abilities, is more important than your reputation. You can't control your reputation. But until you truly understand yourself, your actions, your reputation is on shaky ground. How people perceive you is going to be negative, anyway, if you don't know how to curb your faults.

Forgiveness

My actions and choices hurt my family. I shudder to this day when I think what I put them through. I cringe in horror at how I let them down. The feeling is disabling, and my reaction to my own disgust continued to hurt relationships I was trying to repair. I needed to help myself, to take care of my own emotions before I could work to heal those around me. Would forgiveness really help?

I was desperate for my wife and children to forgive me. I wanted them to tell me that they overlooked my sins and they still loved me, more than ever before. If they told me those things and acted on those words, I would be forever free of the pain that I hurt them.

Except, I had to tell myself the same thing. I needed to forgive myself. I had to grow out of the person I was so I could become the person I was meant to be. But for forgiveness to begin, I needed a reality check. I needed to leave the past in the past, so it didn't ruin today. No, I couldn't change the past. But if I could forgive myself, I could go on.

What steps can you take to forgive yourself?

- Stop beating yourself up. Every time I told myself I was a failure, I reminded myself I forgave myself.

- Take responsibility but don't sit in self-pity. I acknowledged my mistake, but I didn't dwell on it.

- When the past starts to creep up in your memory, actively choose to move on. I quit recalling what happened that night. Sometimes I simply needed to distract myself from the pain and mental replays.

- Get help. I was not afraid to seek professional help if I needed it.

- Allow your experience to fill you with empathy. I was kind to others and more understanding to those with addiction problems.

Rebuilding Means No Excuses

Mentally steady, and emotionally connected to family, I needed to set out to make a stronger effort to get a better job.

But no one would hire me.

And then it struck me. That was just an excuse. I was using "No one will hire me" as an excuse and it was simply not true. They were words I clung to, building a barrier to keep me from getting hurt.

I hadn't regained the weight I lost in prison. I maintained my healthy lifestyle. I began to ask myself, "What about that discipline can help me with other aspects of my life?" I applied the dedication from prison I used when losing weight to other areas of my life. What I learned was a powerful lesson for becoming a gamechanger.

- Quit making excuses. Excuses mean something doesn't get done or fixed.

- Take more responsibility for yourself. I learned I had to clean up my own messes.

- Change your mindset. Be a doer, not a complainer.

- Make the shift to training your mind and body to healthy habits. Train your mind to be successful in everything. Ritually attend the gym. Dress nice. Invest in nice haircuts. Smile.

When you make the extra effort to reject excuses, you step up and outshine your competition. Generally, people aren't willing to better themselves. They just want to skate by with what they know and aren't willing to learn. They are complaining about their life. They don't challenge themselves.

However, not making excuses comes with a heavy price. It means you're in for a fight.

Someone who doesn't make excuses is usually self-made, and you fight the odds against you. You figure life out on your terms, without excuses. You're driven by a mission or a purpose. No matter what, you never lose your determination. Yu are going to make it. No matter what obstacles came to you.

A self-made person who lives without excuses uses every failure as a life lesson—as if it was a steppingstone for what is coming next. Most people see setbacks as the ultimate deterrent, yet I believe we have to go through those things in order to overcome and sharpen our minds.

I knew that if I kept going the way of the clubs, I was heading for destruction. But I took the negative events and learned from them. Some people have three or four DUI's, and their license is suspended or taken away. If you don't learn from those experiences, you are going to go through them again, and the next time is going to be worse.

Someone who is self-made is a person that figures out a way to defy the odds regardless of what obstacles are thrown at them. It is not just a matter of quitting, but persistently fighting for your dream. Put yourself first and keep fighting!

Failing Is Important

Focusing on failing should tell you how important it is. Why? Because, as humans, we avoid failure with all our energy. Yet, if you want to be a gamechanger, you have to risk failure, and you have to learn from failure.

There's a bigger plan for you, and over time, you're going to figure it out. Failing is a part of the process, but people don't like to fail. For example, I invest and lose $10,000. That's okay. $10,000 in my bank is doing nothing. To invest $20,000 with the possibility of making $200,000 is a massive risk, and one I'll take. Most people never make a decision like that. Once you take that leap of faith, you create momentum, and new investment opportunities and advantages present themselves. Your eye is looking for new ways to get ahead and step up. But you won't be able to advance without the risk of failing.

I don't focus on my paycheck anymore. I focus on my opportunities. I take on the risks (responsibly), and the results have been amazing! The paycheck comes, but my job isn't just to work for money—it's to keep advancing myself.

Someone who is self-made is:

- Someone who isn't willing to give up.

- Someone who is going to out-work everyone.

- Someone who loves competition.

- Someone who is up early and ready to work

hard.

- Someone who is drawn toward positive reinforcement and attitude. It's the law of
attraction. The more positive stuff you do the
more positive stuff you will receive.

- Someone who has a big dream mindset.

- Someone who is willing to work extremely
hard. Most people are lazy and just want the
trophy without the work and dedication re-
quired to earn it.

Being unafraid to fail—knowing that there are lessons
in difficulties—will propel you to new heights.

Mastering the Mind

Controlling your thoughts and mind is vital when becoming a gamechanger. Especially when you've had a
setback like mine. I have discovered that many people are
scared to fail, and they are scared of rejection, and terri-
fied of new things. Of course, I think fear is part of the
process. And when you accept fear for what it is, I think
you become unstoppable because you risk failing. And
you fail forward. You fall up toward success. You learn
from it and grow upward.

If you tell yourself that failure is okay, then not all is
lost. It's a win-win, because if you don't win, you still
learn from it. Sure, there is uncertainty. You might have a
season of not having money. It's a scary thing. Yet, a fear
mindset is the opposite of hope. When you're a hopeful
person, you are a positive person. Things come against
you, but you refuse to give in to negativity.

Mastering the mind is controlling how you feel when
things are out of your control. Some people are going to

say things about you, or even to you, that hurt. When it comes to people who are stuck in their mindset and don't want to change, they're not going to like it when you are upbeat and successful. You can't let them get you down. The industry is changing. The world is changing. If you don't change, you are going to be left behind. You are going to be out. To let them control your mindset means you're letting them beat you, so insulate your mind from the naysayers.

In the past, I was very hardheaded and would go crazy on people. I had to learn to master self-control. I realized losing my cool wasn't working. I asked myself, "Why am I being like this?" Now, I take my time and I don't react. I don't get defensive all the time. I go into offense. When bad things come to me, I take my time. And I charge after good things.

What happens when you're cool, calm, and have a strong mindset? You can strategize. You get a different outcome if you're a strategic thinker.

I think that misery loves company. Some people are just miserable, so they want to make other people miserable and unhappy. That's how *they* feel. But you don't have to live a miserable life. Those people can't get to me because my mind is strong, which bothers them even more. I'm choosing to stay strong and keep doing my thing, anyway.

Then, when you've failed your way to success and are strong mentally—but the market turns and sales are low, the government adds taxes, or your business partner is angry—you'll be in a position to keep your cool and play it smart because you've built your life on strong mindfulness.

But even as I was looking for a job and rebuilding my life, I wasn't fulfilled. There was something that I was missing that would complete me. We are made up of mind and body, but I wasn't thinking of my soul.

A complete person is mentally and physically strong, but the one element missing was my spirituality. I needed to make a decision that would impact the rest of my life.

WORKBOOK

Chapter Five Questions

Question: Does your family come before your career? If so, how do you demonstrate that? What would your children say if they were asked which you value more? Are there areas where you need to rebuild trust and relationships within your family, and how can you do so through talk and time?

_____

_____

_____

_____

_____

_____

_____

_____

_____

Question: What excuses do you hold on to for your lack of success or your ongoing problems? How can you begin to take responsibility for your mistakes? What healthy habits and disciplines do you need to work into your life?

_____

_____

_____

_____

_____

_____

_____

_____

_____

_____

_____

Action: In what ways do you fear risk and/or failure? Write out a list of the fears that hold you back. Now beside each one write a motivational truth statement that will help you to develop a strong mind even in the midst of setbacks.

Example:

Fear: I fear not meeting my goals and consequently not having enough to pay my bills.

Motivator: Through learning to manage my finances wisely, I can adjust my lifestyle to live on less and save up for lean seasons.

Chapter Five Notes

CHAPTER SIX

Routines

Sometimes, a person needs more motivation than consequences. You need to understand the cosmic role you play in the universe to keep you grounded and focused. Understanding a stronger Being than you reflects in your daily habits and actions. Especially when you understand the power God is eager to give you.

Here's my problem, and the issue most people have. While they know that there is a God, they hate attending church services. And I was one of them. As a kid, I thought church was boring. I didn't learn to pray, I never learned the songs, and understanding the homilies was out of the question—I didn't listen.

Would you say a person chooses God? Or does God choose you? I believe He chooses you. He chose me, and it changed my life.

A New Perspective: Helping Others

As soon as I left prison, I tried to make a go of things. I managed to reconnect with my wife and kids, along with my extended family and friends. The job search felt pointless, but at least I was heading the right direction.

My brother's wife talked my brother into attending church, and he jumped in headfirst, becoming born again and following Christ. They were so excited, my parents followed them to church and converted. Not just in name. They all turned toward Christ.

My parents and brother turned their attentions to me and my wife. They kept pushing for us to attend church with them. They wouldn't let up. I told my wife we had to go to church, or we would never hear the end of it. But I didn't want to go to church for two hours. It sounded like a nightmare. Sitting there with religious stuff going on mindlessly was more than I could handle.

But we decided to go. It was from 11 to 2 o'clock, and I prepped my mind for a ridiculously boring time.

Something happened that day that is hard to explain. It wasn't coincidence that I picked that day to go. God chose for me to go. As I sat in the seats and listened and watched what was going on—my heart thumped in my chest, and my mind spun with the truth that was laid before us. I turned to my wife and whispered. "Do you feel what I feel?

She nodded.

It was a different experience. I felt a gravity from the truth and the meaning coming from it, and I needed to stay close to it. I wanted to find out more. No one had taught me about God the way this pastor taught. I started there. We kept going. We brought the kids to church every Sunday, and we became members of the church. I felt like there was a different atmosphere there.

One day, I realized I was acting a little different. I kind of liked it. This was it. This was an answer to my bigger questions, "Why am I on this planet?" We were all baptized—my wife and the kids.

Christ has changed my life forever.

I am not perfect. We are all sinners every day. But God has so much mercy for us. And I ask Him every Sunday,

"Why me?"

You may feel like you don't deserve it. He has a reason. Everything is for His glory. It's the reason why we are here.

I fail every day, even though I strive to be the best version of myself. In a perfect world, my efforts would be applauded. But not always in the car business. Some people don't like a push for the best. And for me, that means checking on what the Lord would have of me.

I'll find myself in a situation and I look up and ask God what I should do in that situation. I pray about every project. Sometimes I get confirmation—sometimes I don't. There is a reason why I am reaching out to Him. God put me in this situation. He put me in the car business. Of course, if He wants me to do something else, He will make a way. And not only am I going to check in with Him, I am going to share with the world to give Him the glory.

What God Did for Me

I have a personal relationship with God. What does that mean? He lives in me. And all who pray and have Christ in them, have a different strength God has gifted them, which gives them a different view. But how could I live a selfish life? I follow the commandments. It's the truth that Christ died for me to save me (John 3:16). And the only way to go to God is to go through Jesus Christ (John 14:6). So, I follow Him.

People look at religion and they take it to the extreme. How can I be a Christian? People get so caught up in what people and the world are going to say. However, God loves you no matter what, and for who you are. No person is perfect, and He still loves you.

Because the spiritual aspect of my life is so important,

I:

- Pray every morning.
- Thank God for another day.
- Leave difficult situations up to God.
- Pray in public, even if people look at me weird.
- Go to church every Sunday.

And I'm blessed. And I thank God for what He's doing, not just what it is doing to me, but for my kids. Twenty years from now they will have their own family, and they are going to be in church, because daddy took them to Church. They are going to have following Christ as their norm, and they will be in Church. I'm leading by example.

When I was little, I wasn't made to go to Church, and I wish I was. My parents and Grandma were Catholic. I wasn't faithfully attending mass. But now, I feel good when I go to church and get on my knees to pray after a long, hard week. I pray for my enemies and the people who come against me. I sometimes go alone because my wife can't go. Even when we are away, we will go to church with kids. Why? Because we don't want to miss out. Wanting to be there makes all the difference in the world.

The God Effect

When I became a believer in Jesus Christ, I felt a strong urge to give back to the community and the world. There were emotions tugging at my heart. What could I do to help others?

My church had a powerful way to feed the poor and care for the sick—missions. Simply put, missions is sending people over to offer a helping hand for the less fortunate. I turned to my original skillset that I had thought through as a youth. I could speak two languages, and I was a salesman.

I started to do missions in poor countries. Taking a moment to reflect, I had gone from a kid in El Salvador hanging out with friends and getting in trouble, to an ambassador for Christ in other countries. This is the kind of change Christ makes. I had a heart that was willing to do better. And I wanted to share Christ with everyone. I had become born again, and it made all the difference.

But with my sales background, I had to decide how vocal to be about my faith. We live in a society where you have to be very careful with your words. You get a label of biased or racist with your words. I decided to be bold. Now, I mention God and give Him praise without hesitation. I put God first. Now, people talk about how I am Christian. Just like in car sales, when someone is excited about the product, they want to talk about it.

When I looked to the higher power and the Truth that is Christ, I cringe that my past was filled with blindness.

I have been to Honduras, Santo Domingo, and Peru. I have plans to help build a church in Spain.

Memories of my life in El Salvador flash in my mind as I work in missions. When I was little, people came to my hometown with huge plastic containers. They would pop the lids, reach inside, and hand out clothes and food. They gave away a lot of stuff for Christmas. Everyone got a shirt or pants or shoes. Mostly it was clothing, outdated stuff from the United States but a new outfit for us. Everyone was excited because we would have new clothes to wear for Christmas. It lifted our spirits and made us so happy. I remember wearing those clothes and now I want to have the same impact on people there. I always like to give back. It comes back to you ten times.

The kindness impacted me. We eagerly waited and

watched for the trucks with the gifts to come. I want to be that person, the driver, who people look forward to coming. I want to impact those kids that live in places like my hometown. In fact, I want to return to my hometown and bless them as I have been blessed.

The visits help families more than you might think. And yet, it helps me as well. When I go to those countries, I come back a different person. I take care of people. I want them to know the world's okay, that they will be oaky.

There are local works we do as well. We feed about one-hundred families in Brooklyn, just to be a blessing to those around us. Many of these folks depend on us and our business to feed their families. What a blessing!

So, how do missions work? Basically, you go with a group from your church, and your group meets up with different groups from other churches. You fly to an orphanage, or you go to a school, settle in, and get to work.

In Santo Domingo, there were one hundred kids we fed, played with, and taught. And we gave them basic need items and toys. Sadly, these kids were abandoned by the parents, and yet, there are churches there that teach these kids for free. And we don't just bring them gifts and toys, but we teach them songs and teach them dances. We spent an entire week with those kids.

Peru was kind of the same thing. The country is so poor. We brought in fifty beds and stoves, baskets of food, barrels of medical supplies, and other odds and ends. The pastor of the area knew the needs of the people and helped us distribute the right goods to the right families. In the end, we visited ten churches. We were fortunate enough to give our testimony in hopes it would impact someone. Seeds of truth got planted there. This area staggered me. It was so poor. There was no food or water. You come back and realize what you have. It makes you want to give more.

In Spain, there are a lot of Catholics. However, most don't attend church, so the pastor I'm working with is a bit more creative. He is creating a café for patrons to enjoy coffee throughout the week. Toward the back of the café, they are building a church. True, his idea is unorthodox. Some don't like him because he thinks outside the box. Yet, he has to be different to attract people.

Naturally, he is having some issues with funds, and I pray I will be able to help him out. It could be labor, or financially, or sharing my word. When it comes to missions, almost anything goes. Whatever they need you do. It's Christ driven—it always goes back to Christ so that He can change their lives.

Missions taught me:

- How to stay grounded.

- To be humble.

- To be appreciative of all the things I have.

- To never forget where I come from.

- Not to be greedy.

- The more you make the more you give.

- Giving changes people for the better.

- Missions is a great way to bond with your children.

- To make memories with my family.

Missions Skillset

I am a positive guy. There are some days I have bad days. I don't like to be depressed. If I had a bad day at work, I am going to talk about it until we make it right.

Today wasn't a very good day sales wise but it was a productive day. I accomplished other things, just not sales.

When it comes to missions, you can't mope and be depressed. You have to be positive, offering hope despite the conditions around you. But it has to be real. Honest. You have to really feel upbeat or they'll know you're lying.

It means that you are real and authentic. You are realistic when you say you're fortunate. To counteract the depression around me, it means being grateful for what I have. Family. Skillsets. Ways and means. However, it's bad out there. For many, the world truly is ending, and they just need love and attention. Being real to the situation is knowing there is an issue and real about what you have, or the situation defines you.

This also means you have to take care of yourself. I use the gym and have a trainer. It keeps me physically and mentally active, and I'm able to stay focused on the tasks I must do, between dealership work, helping around the house, and missions. I must be strong and fit, mind and body, or I won't be able to be the person others need.

Before missions, I was just status quo—a guy trying to make my way in the world. Sure, I was a talented guy. But I didn't have discipline or work ethic. I lacked the discipline to take it to the next level. I think missions are the reason why my focus increased drastically. So many are dependent on me. And I think the discipline and energy transfers to the next person. I think that I wasn't as productive. I worked twelve hours a day, but I didn't get anything done. I wasn't being productive. Being involved with missions taught me how to maximize my time. I learned to not be a know-it-all and to be a student of sales. I learned to expand myself and to go higher.

As is generally stated, if your dreams don't scare you, get a bigger dream. It's about the challenge. If it makes sense, I will go for it. People don't realize how powerful the mindset is. It will change your whole life. Missions did that for me.

Overcoming Personal Challenges

I believe in the law of attraction. I believe in positive reinforcement and energy. And if you keep spreading that positive energy, that positive energy is going to come back to you. But that doesn't mean everything is going to be great all the time.

It's easy to be negative in the car business, because salesmen in the car business have a negative stigma. The reason why I started out in car sales and now this book project is I wanted to change that negativity stigma. What I realized is that the law of attraction brings positivity toward you. You keep saying consciously positive things in your mind, and it starts pulling positive toward you. I know it works, because it happened for me.

I don't use words like depressed because the words you speak become life. When you speak a negative word, it becomes real. The power is in the tongue. If I'm having a bad day, I'm going to just say I'm a bit down, but I don't say I am depressed. Changing your mindset and changing the way you think is important. Your old self will tell you to be negative. But with a negative mindset, you are not going to get anywhere. If you start believing the negative, it becomes reality. If you say you are going to be a boozer all your life, keep saying it, that's what you are going to be. And if you keep repeating negative things, the universe is going to find a way to accept that you're a loser. But it's changeable. Be positive.

Be positive with your income. Be positive with your health. Have faith everything is going to be better.

When a customer spends a lot of time trying to decide on a car, and I've missed out on three really good customers, and then the one I'm with doesn't buy, I used to get angry. Or when a coworker says I stole their customer, or a buyer asks for more once the deal is done, it used to bother me. I used to get angry a lot, but now I have learned how to control my emotions.

So, when someone confronts me or approaches me and I'm tempted to lash out right back at them, or simply have a tantrum, I walk away after the person says what they have to say. I don't make emotional decisions anymore. I can't keep losing sales and opportunities because I can't control my temper. If someone comes to me and lashes out. I just stay quiet. And you would be surprised how much more it messes them up.

When someone is angry with me, I stay quiet and I go home. Then I study why it happened. Why did that take place? What was the reason behind it? How can it be prevented next time? What can I learn from this?

But you should only think through events when you are in a calm state of mind. If you are in a bad state, you are going to make bad decisions that you'll regret the next day. I even do it in my close relationships. People make things bigger than they really are, and if you give them a little time, chances are, they'll calm down and you can have a rational conversation.

Is Materialism Fulfilment?

We all have dreams. Some want to hold a position in a business, like vice president or CEO, because they've been called a nobody before. Wealth drives others, perhaps because they had to do without as youth and they don't want their family to go through the same. Or maybe you don't want to be a millionaire. That's fine. It's your prerogative. Everyone is different. We all have different goals for different reasons, but one thing is clear: materialism, the desire to be someone or have things, is no one's end goal. There's a reason deeper than just wanting things that drives a person.

For example, I'm getting other things out of my desire to rise to the top. For me, money is the byproduct of a drive for personal best. With that comes a title. While it may look like materialism, my drive for personal best makes me try new challenges, expand my knowledge, and focus on perfection. I'll keep driving. The result is people putting me in important positions in the company, and the pay reflects that. What looks like materialism is simply the benefits of being my best.

I believe that if you aren't striding high, then you hit low. If you want to challenge yourself, you have to be unrealistic. That's right: unrealistic. That means stretching yourself and the limits of your work far beyond what you think you're capable of. You have to think outside of the box. That's why I am in the position I'm in today.

When you strive to be your best, people will look at you like you are crazy. You are greedy. Honestly, it's a valid assumption. But they're wrong. There's enough pie in this world for everyone. I want a slice big enough to share with others. So, you have to respect your naysayers. Feel good about their jealousy. I'm not working to keep them happy. I keep doing it because it works for me and I get paid doing it and I enjoy it.

Another angle is that we are all materialistic we just don't admit it on camera. True, money isn't everything, but what can you do for the poor if you aren't gathering in enough resources? While it's not just about money, I am doing it for the other things. I work hard to give my kids the best life they can have. My dad worked a lot to make sure I had a good life. If you work overtime so you can put food on the table, you're working for material things. And I salute you.

When you are focusing on the paycheck, you are living paycheck to paycheck. You are so focused on the fact that you never have money. Your mind doesn't expand that there are other opportunities out there, so you just keep working hard doing the same things.

Some people think working eighty hours a week is all about the value. What does value mean here? How does working so many hours actually benefit you? It's not just about eighty hours on a time clock. You could be watching social media for eighty hours at work and still not be productive. If you bring value to any company, you can change things around, which goes hand in hand with the opportunities, which are endless. If you focus on your paycheck weekly, you are always going to be broke. You're being materialistic. You are always going to be living paycheck to paycheck instead of focusing on moving the company in the right direction and getting everyone going the same way.

Once I believed I could sell a quick three hundred cars. It was my vision. Everyone was wondering how? We have never done those numbers. I stood firm. That's the goal. That's what we are going to do. If I sell three hundred cars, I am going to make a ton of money, but I'm not focused on that. I am just focused on hitting the goal, a personal goal I set for myself. And I never lower my goals. My goals are always the same and more. It's detrimental if you lower your goals.

Don't care about the money. Pretend you take off for a few months, and someone on your crew makes a massive change and it brings in more lookers, but the money is the same, this guy has got a lot of value. People are so focused on the paycheck and not realizing that building by value and bringing more to the table, there is a lot of potential to make a lot more than you were. It's about the possibility of sales that you can take advantage of in many cases, helping your company name get out there.

I worked at a Toyota dealership, I worked for top brands like Ford, and I never made close to the amount of money I make now. Not even close. so that goes to tell you the brand has nothing to do with it. It's the value that you bring.

Anytime you start a new job at a dealership, they put you on a payment plan, which is what you are going to make. What percentage of the store are you going to get? What is your salary? If you bring in X amount, what are you going to make off your sales? Most are more focused on their payment plan before they start the job. I went the opposite. I told them don't give me a payment plan, just let me see what I can do first.

They thought I was overconfident. People thought I was cocky. I wasn't. My mission trips had taught me that materialism isn't the end goal, and I needed to play smarter than that. There's a difference between being confident and being cocky. I was able to negotiate what I wanted and then some. And then I put them on the map nationally. True, I only wanted to do it in Brooklyn. Now the whole country knows who they are. They're in all sorts of magazine articles.

I can now approach the owners, telling them that you will sell a hundred cars if you invest in someone. It's the same as saying, "Hey listen, I'm going to charge you $100,000 next month, but you are going to double in sales, and at about $4,000 a sale—$4,000 dollars times one hundred cars is $400,000 in profit. I pay myself the money I make because it's the money I generate. I double the sales, so I need the piece of the pie that belongs to me. And that's where materialism comes in. Some people might think you make too much money, but you earned it. No one sees what it takes to get there; all they see is the final paycheck. And then, sometimes they ignore or don't see how you use your money to help others.

But that's okay. You have to rise above these criticisms and search for fulfillment.

Fulfillment Is More Important Than Being Happy

Happiness is a state of mind. You can be happy with anything. I was happy when I was money poor but rich in friends. However, some things get old. The novelty wears off and runs out when the money comes in and you can afford amazing things. Sure, you see all these things you accomplish. But that wears off as well.

Fulfillment is the person you become while in the pursuit of happiness. To me, fulfillment is having security and confidence. It means trusting in my talent and understanding the people I work for, enough that I'm not worried about my job. As someone who grew accustomed to depending only on myself in the past, I've found that a good job is important to my sense of satisfaction with life.

Being Relentless

Missions taught me there is only one way to help others: to be relentless in all you do. If you don't know how to do something, you just say, "Yes, I will do that," then go figure it out.

What does a relentless person look like?

- They are willing to do the things that others aren't willing to do.

- When they fall, they get back up.

- They may be confronted with one million ideas, but they act on the best one.

- They're okay with changing their life over one great idea.

- Stopping is not an option.

- Failure is just a redirection.

- They read. A lot.

- They understand if people don't know your name, then you aren't doing nothing.

- They don't give up.

- They find another way.

- They deal with problems on a daily basis and don't ignore difficult issues.

- They try a different way and figure it out by the end of the day.

My kids are watching what I am doing. They will know if I'm not doing my best.

Sometimes, being relentless is exhausting. How do you keep going when you're tired? Passion is the answer. You have to find out why you want this. Why do you want to be successful so badly? I want to be the best. I want to be like that guy or woman who is rising, because if you're not going up, you're being passed, and that means you're going down.

Find a life coach. Their counsel helps. They will spot weak areas in your life and in your thinking, as well as pointing out your skills and where you excel.

Once you get to the top, the relentless part is staying on top. You have to keep working hard to stay there. A thousand people are trying to get my spot. If you are number one, you are thinking who is number two. It takes a huge number of hours on social media to stay on top. You've got to train your salespeople to be the best as well. It looks easy, but if you aren't relentless, you aren't going to stay on top. Your value goes down.

Money Versus Opportunity

People focus on the money all the time. I used to be that person. I used to live paycheck to paycheck. Most of my career in the car business was paycheck to paycheck, so I was focused on the pay and on what I make and this and that. Then it occurred to me that if I want to make a million dollars, I had to find the opportunity to make the million dollars I so badly wanted. But I was going to get it.

My thinking process was a huge mistake. I was playing to a number and not focusing on opportunities.

When someone gives you an opportunity and you don't focus on the dollar, and you go all in to bring value to that company, the money takes care of itself. Be the best version of yourself, and eventually you are going to get paid more than what you are working for.

I used to work extremely hard, and I never made the money I am making now. Now, I have a very good life. I work hard because I choose to go all in.

Now, don't get me wrong. Don't be used by someone. You should get kickbacks for your success. Money should be important, but not your main motivation. Money shouldn't be your number-one reason for working hard. It locks you down. It holds you back from taking risks and going for opportunities. Rather, focus on opportunity. I focus on the opportunities that come to me now and money is just flowing like crazy. Don't chase after dollars; chase after opportunities. If you're petty about every dime, you'll just be chasing money, but millions will pass over your head to the people who have the opportunities.

I do a lot of things that I don't charge for. Not just missions. In business. I do things because I want to do it. The customers I work with think they're getting a deal. And they are. But in the future, that money's going to come back to me ten times over. If you build a relationship, everyone wants to do business with you.

Chase the opportunity, not the money.

In the end, life's a process. I'm in love with the process. Other people want the trophy or the ring. They don't want to put in the work. While I'm one of the most successful GMs in the country, and people want to hang out with winners because they want the energy, the fame and fortune aren't the important things. It's really about the process that it took to get here.

Even though I had captured a job and was working hard to rebuild my reputation and to give back to the community, I wasn't where I needed to be. I wasn't a gamechanger. I would need to work even harder to make the changes that would land me and my family in the most successful positions in car sales. I can't wait to share with you how I did it.

WORKBOOK

Chapter Six Questions

Question: Does faith inform and inspire your business decisions? If not, how could a relationship with God and a focus on giving back to others make a difference in your life? What are some needs either locally or globally that you feel drawn to help meet?

_____

_____

_____

_____

_____

_____

_____

_____

_____

_____

Question: Is your focus on your paycheck or on being and doing your best with the opportunities you have? What are your dreams and goals? Would others call them "unrealistic" or have you settled for good enough? Why do you want what you want—what is the ultimate driving motivator behind your desire to succeed?

_____

_____

_____

_____

_____

_____

_____

_____

_____

_____

_____

Action: For a few days practice listening to yourself. Write down the words and phrases that you say or think often. How are you describing yourself, your life, your family, your skills, your job? Are you speaking primarily positively or negatively? Are your mindset and words self-defeating or relentless?

_____

_____

_____

_____

_____

_____

_____

_____

_____

_____

_____

_____

Chapter Six Notes

CHAPTER SEVEN

Strategies

I am the founder of the Automotive Game Changer Conference. Over 270 energetic people attended in Long Island, far more than expected, so we scrambled for more room, more chairs, more everything. Because I was eager to give back to the community that gave so much to me, I made sure this event was top notch.

I paid for everything. First off, I wanted to prove to everyone it could be done, not just with the money and resources, but with the time my success afforded me. I booked the rooms and food. And we put it together so quickly, everyone was shocked. Secondly, I wanted people to understand that this is a team effort. We're in this together. We can help each other reach our potential if we share tips and chat about our work.

It was one of the best days of my life. The conference was so rewarding. The day meant so much to me. My daughter went up on stage, and she had a bit of stage fright. She marched up to the microphone and tearing up said she was very proud of her dad. My kids were proud of me. It was a highlight moment in my life.

Thinking outside of the box, I was the first dealership ever to put on a conference. Some of the side benefits were that people wanted to partner with me. You'll have validation if you are seen with him.

The next conference I'm hosting will be bigger and other industries will be involved

What did it take for me, a man who nearly lost everything in prison, to rising in business and living the high life?

The Wall

I sat down in my office one day and planned my future. I realized if I didn't have a goal, something to focus on, I couldn't plan. What did I want?

I wanted to have eight franchises total.

That was a tall order. How much would I need to make this year? One million dollars by the end of the year would put me in a good place.

I paused. Grant Cardone in his book *The 10X Rule*, recommends you take your goal, and do it times ten.[1] I grabbed my checkbook and a pen and scribbled out a check. Ten million dollars, written to me. To be cashed at the end of the year.

I took a pin, walked over to the office wall, and pinned up the check as a constant reminder of what I was working for.

The check represents the skills and activities I'm going to focus on to reach my goal. What is it going to take to earn that check?

- Be the best in the automotive industry.

- Be the guy who wants to learn from.

- Stay focused on affording some toys.

- Be *the* marketing guy, and everyone knows it.

- Don't let up. Be relentless.

Don't apologize for wanting things. When you pin your goal to the wall, it doesn't need an explanation for anyone. For example, I want to have a car for every day of the week. Now, I can't drive all seven cars at one time, but I want a garage with seven cars, and I can pick a car for a different day. To me that is freedom. The ultimate financial goal for me is I want to drive expensive cars whenever I want. I am not there yet, and I have a lot of work to do. I am just getting started. I'd happily settle for what I have right now, but I want to challenge myself even more. I want to be able to look at my wall when I'm growing tired, and realize I still have work to do. With a goal on the wall, you just have to look up.

Dream big. If your dream doesn't scare, you need a bigger dream. But then be a doer. Put massive action behind the dream. When you put your effort out there in the world, the universe will bring it back to you.

Be the marketing genius. Work hard so that when you are working for the underdog, it's a big deal. It turns heads. When you're the marketing guru, small companies will pull their resources to bring you on, and you can make waves. They say, "Hey, what could the guy do at a Honda store?" And when the marketing genius moves, he takes his wall with him or her. Why? Because no matter how high he takes the business. He's going to rise with it.

I've been the guy who had the worst brand in the country but was successful anyway, with great management skills and fantastic sales numbers. If I could do it with such an insignificant brand, what is your excuse? Stop making justifications. The brand is what it is. The customer knows what it is. Now I'm pushing Mitsubishi, a quality brand and business. But I showed my worth and am always progressing in my skills. I still have a wall with a goal.

When I didn't have a wall, it's not that I was a bad salesman, but I was arrogant and undirected. Perhaps I am still a bit arrogant. But people confused my confidence with arrogance. I know where I am going and what I'm about. And people take that as cockiness and judge me for it.

What challenge can't I take on? I am never going to say no. And neither should you. I am never going to say it's impossible. Go out, figure out the answers, and come back with numbers to show you can do anything. It's okay to brag as long as you can back up with your numbers. You can to talk smack as long as you're number one on the board. But I don't put that on my wall. It's just the check, the one goal.

Be confident. Have the numbers to back it up. If you are putting 110% in, then expect to be the best. Make big promises and over-deliver to bring that value. I did it in the whole country. I built the brand. Therefore, the money will come naturally. When they pay you the crazy money with extra sources of income coming in and people want to partner with you, you know you're on the right track.

Sales Strategies That Work

I am known as *the* car dealer, the marketing king. I'm the gamechanger, the powerhouse. I'm not bragging, just saying what people call me. My strategy is to be very aggressive. What is aggressive selling?

- Guerilla marketing means being in the customer's face. Have the product front and center for the customer to keep focused on. Don't let them look away.

- Be better than your competition. Don't skimp with your campaigns. Go all in. Be a louder voice, flashier picture, better product.

- Stay five steps ahead. Get a feel for what the

customers will be looking for tomorrow and push those agendas.

- Keep your skills up. Train on a weekly basis. Read or listen to books every second you can. Go to conferences on a monthly basis on the industry. Always learning, always finding new things, always open minded.

- Give the customer leverage to negotiate and take part in dealings and give the customers a better experience.

- Don't let the things that go wrong cut into your pitch. Just go with it.

- Make phone calls and emails during down times.

- Stay with a vendor for years. I'm never satisfied with only one or two vendors.

- Come every day with every ounce of energy to take it to the next level.

The world is evolving daily, sometimes hourly, and if you're not up with the times or current, you'll be left behind. I'm 90 percent digital with my strategies because that's where the industry is, where the customers are hanging out. That means your customers are so much more educated than ever before. They can look up any scrap of information while they're talking to you. Never let on you believe the customer is dumb. In fact, people will pay for a more streamlined person, a person who is respectful, and a good experience. There is a demand for a convenience.

When you pay attention to things and stay above and current with the industry, you will stay alive, no matter what the economy is doing. You will keep the customer for life. The people want to be treated the right way.

Taking a Stand for Yourself

The first way of taking a stand for yourself is maximizing your pay. You deserve to be taken care of. But you also need to take risks first to show your worth.

There are two pay plans for a car salesman. He or she can take a draw on commission on future sales, meaning if the dealer pays the new salesman up front to get by for a bit, it goes against the salesman's future commission. The rate isn't great. The other way is to just go with commission, so sometimes it takes a while for the pay to start rolling in.

I walked into a dealer and looked at the lot. I saw they had six-hundred or more cars in stock. I asked for ninety days to see what I could do to unload the heavy inventory. I wanted nothing in writing. No payment plan for ninety days. I was going to make them rich. I pushed cars, sending them home with happy customers. And the dealer was working hard to restock. When the ninety days were up and it was time to sit down to talk money, I was in the driver's seat.

Look at the opportunity, not the money. Look over the lot to see what you are working with. Make an offer based on your situation. Then, once you give them a taste of what you can do, they will give you whatever you want. The numbers keep crawling up. You can negotiate with leverage. Once you show them a taste of how fast inventory can move, they won't say no to you. I have done that at two stores. At one, it took me seven months to put a deal together. In this case, the dealer was limited to fewer than four hundred cars. I rolled up my sleeves, and it was a matter of getting a way of it done. I brought in my tools and went to work.

There's a catch to the dealer. I like to do it my way: my team, my way, and my rules. That way, it has a stamp of personal touch. Direct control. I suggest you do the same. Don't allow anyone to micromanage you. If you can't be who are, then it simply won't work for you. It must flow from you, and customers will connect with your personal charisma.

If you're a dealer, what's the point of hiring someone unique if you already have it figured out? You already tried that recipe, but it didn't work. Just buy someone's time and plug them into your system, and good luck. But it works better if you give me the keys and give me a budget. It's exactly what Brooklyn did. And now they're well known.

Do it your way. It has the biggest payoff. 2018 was the most profitable sales market in twenty years. I pay myself. I pay myself on commission. I doubled their business and I pay myself from the excess spoils of success. I generated that money. In the car business, there is no limit on what I make.

The second way to care for yourself is to make yourself happy by paying yourself first. After all the risks, reap the rewards. If you've a team under you, inspire them by making sure you're well taken care of. And you need to be happy and have a good attitude. If you aren't happy you are going to be miserable. And miserable salespeople don't sell. Please yourself and pay yourself first.

People don't love themselves. Love yourself first. Your goals are important and shouldn't be tossed away just because someone is jealous. My happiness is not just about fulfillment. I ask myself, is this going to make me happy? Is this going to give me financial freedom? Will this give my family a better life? Some people aren't going to like that. That's where the haters come in. When it comes down to it, it's only you against the world. They aren't going to be there for you when things go south.

When some people are your friend only to use your popularity, and you know who is being fake and playing the game, you must take care of yourself first.

The third way of taking care of yourself is creating a culture you are comfortable in. Culture is very important. I walked into a dealership and the vibes were so negative, I almost walked out. It came from the top. The GM was negative, and it spread to everyone. The guy would come in there at 2 o'clock in the afternoon and start yelling and screaming at everyone. No one wanted to be productive.

If you're the boss, you must lead by example. But if you are walking in at 1 or 2 o'clock in the afternoon and calling the shots, no one is going to look at you as a leader. You've got to be a leader, or you will never succeed. If the people hate their jobs and the environment, and are dreading being there, the bad culture is going to permeate to the customer, which means no sales.

If the cancer starts from the top, guess what is going to happen at the bottom? It's going to spread quickly, and a broken culture will be the status quo. Bad customer service, no relationship with the banks, all because you are the boss. It's about building those relationships and changing culture into a positive one, where everyone is happy to work together. A GM should come in there with a mindset that say, "As a team, we are going to make things happen." The guy who washes the car is as important as the woman who owns the place. Treat everyone with respect and everyone at every level like they are important to the company, and the company is going to flourish.

I took the leadership part and wrestled the negativity into positivity. There is no negativity in my way. Some stuff I have to be real about and make some decisions that are difficult, which is just part of the job. It doesn't mean my mind turns into a pit of negativity and ruins the whole day. I just make the hard decisions and move the company onward.

Culture is vital to a company. Culture is the most important thing in any business. It's the vibes a customer gets when they step on the lot. And not just in the car business but in any business. If you have to fire your top guy to get the culture right, then you have to fire your top guy, especially if they are creating a bully atmosphere. They've got to go. If they aren't willing to change, you have to cut them lose. One person in leadership can make or break you.

When I took over the position of the negative GM, one of the owners was on vacation. There was a hostile takeover of the dealer. I came in and wondered what was going on. I started working and watching the GM before taking his position. I saw the culture and its negative affect on the company.

I started making changes, and by ninety days, I had started hiring new people to replace the old people, who were loyal to the previous, lackluster GM. But most watched me, this new guy who had a new way, and they were eager to try it my way. Some had been set in their ways for the past twenty years, and sales were slumping. I let people go, and the sales went to the sky. That one GM had been hurting the entire operation.

What happens if people challenge your authority? What if they say, my way or the highway? You must take a different approach. I go with the approach that the positive theme is better for the team. I draw everyone together and tell them, "Listen, the punter is just as important as the quarterback." I continue with the team theme. I use baseball and basketball analogies, because they are relatable to businesses as well. Everyone loves a comeback story, but everyone must be going for the same goal. Then the team is unstoppable. My way or the highway doesn't work.

To sum up the three areas of taking a stand for yourself,

you must do things your way to maximize your payoff, then pay yourself first, and finally, you must create your culture, which includes a positivity that makes people want to work for you. They will love you for it. They will go out of their way for you. And if you find their loyalty is strong, embrace that.

Most GM and owners believe in fear. Fear is a good motivator, but it doesn't last long. Fear is a feeling that doesn't last for a long time. It doesn't give you loyalty or inspire them to be better.

If all this sounds like a lot of work, remember, I made a career out of this job. I made myself a millionaire without a high school education. I figured it out and I am not smarter than you. If you take that approach and inspire others and be positive about it all, the sky is the limit.

Motivating Tactics, with Occasional Discipline

You want to motivate your workers. Push them hard with motivation. But first, you must have motivation in your own life. If it's possible, show them that you can have a job in sales and have financial freedom, by leading with your example. If you really become a gamechanger, it takes energy. They'll take your energy and become gamechangers themselves.

- If they work really hard and put in the hours, reward them with kind words.

- Can you find room in the budget for deeper discounts on their car purchases based on their sales?

- Team meetings with statistics are a great way to help motivate their sales numbers.

- One on one training makes people feel special.

- Helping with a sale and telling them good job will cement in their mind how to follow your style.

Sometimes, no matter how much you do to work with an employee, you have to use discipline. It's a sad truth, but some people don't need a carrot to propel them, but a stick. Consider the options of what to do with a toxic employee carefully, so that their negativity doesn't pass to others.

The following are some of the many options.

- Simply cut out the cancer. You can spend time with them, but if they don't believe in your vision and they become haters, they must go. Remember, we're working for a positive atmosphere, not negative.

- Consider making an example of them. Sometimes you must expose their attitude, their actions, or their lack of attention to the job. Call them out on stuff they are doing. Some get the message when called out because people can jump on a wagon, for good or for bad. And calling them out is an attempt to create a good, functional wagon.

- Work with them, giving them more attention than is normal. This can run counter to the positivity by creating jealousy, so watch the reactions of the other employees.

- When everyone is trying to do their best while an employee is bringing everyone else down, point it out to the employee. But do it privately. Even your best employee can drive the company to the brink of failure, and they might need to be told they're toxic.

- Ask them privately what's the agenda behind their actions. It creates an open environment to talk, and maybe get things back on track.

- If you feel or sense an employee pulling away, they may turn into bit of a hater. Maybe they're jealous. Maybe you are more successful than them. They are turning against you. They secretly want to be you, but they can't. It may be time to let them go.

The Mindset of Problematic Employees

Words are powerful, and whatever you say or write in an email will affect your relationship with the person, for good or for bad. It can make or break a relationship. So, you must be careful with what you say. When you notice a problem with an employee, be careful on how you approach them. What is their mindset?

Some are eager to maintain a status quo, to just do their time at a job. These people have given up on life. They're just trying to get enough money to buy a little entertainment, and that's the end. They're not eager enough to excel and learn how to rise. That's why people aren't successful because they get defeated. This mindset slows them down and drags the team down. But you can rock the ship by working harder and breaking from the normal and the safe. You're looking for employees that are interested in taking care of themselves by investing in the company, because they know the richer they make the company, the richer they will get. These personal goals simply help everyone.

Another mindset is discipline. I disciplined myself to eat right, to make sacrifices, to wake up at 5 o'clock in the morning, and I'm in the best shape of my life. I can give it my best all day because I have the energy, because I had the discipline to work hard. If you cry and pout all the time guess what? You are going to be broke all the time. You're going to lose the drive because if you're pouting and complaining, you're going to believe yourself. You got to stop believing you are a loser. The world will give you positivity if you offer it positivity as well. But that takes discipline.

Sometimes, an employee feels sorry for themselves. Some of the reasons might be that they feel like they are settling for a sales job when they really want to be an artist. Or they married the wrong person, and they drag the negative emotions to the workplace. These people aren't happy, and they end up putting their sadness onto other people. They aren't happy where they are, and they inadvertently make everyone else just as miserable. If you're happy all the time, it seems to make them angrier, and they work harder to drag people under the mud with them.

Everyone gets down, but some just can't bounce back up. If something bad happens, it ruins their whole day. In reality, it was just one bad thing, and the whole day goes by with plenty of good things, and yet, they let the one negative event spoil the day. Don't let them live there. Just move on. It's not going to ruin my day, nor the other employees' day.

Discipline Is Key

From morning to night, controlling your life decisions makes you who you are. This takes strict discipline. What does that look like in my life?

Suffering makes me feel like a champion. What does that mean? The harder we push our bodies, the more our bodies adjust to the new environment. Now, you can overdo it. But the majority of people don't push themselves at all.

I don't want to be the kind of guy that is going to work till 67 and only enjoy my life for eleven years because it will be over by 78. What kind of life is that? I want to retire in ten years. That means discipline. I want to retire in ten years and enjoy the rest of my life—and still give my kids and my family the best life that I can give them. I want to enjoy my life now. I'm going to discipline myself and do what I've got to do to make that happen.

I am young and have the energy to maximize large amounts of hours. If I am up before 5:30 in the morning and work one hundred hours a week, whatever it takes a person to do in a year, I am doing in three months. I'm ahead of you. That takes discipline—serious discipline.

A boss told an employee that he was going to fire him if he didn't file all of his reports. It sounded like a random ultimatum, as if he was trying to challenge the employee. We can get complacent and people don't like change. However, to do the reports would help the company. It would just take discipline. So, don't ask, "Why is this guy doing this or that?" Take the time and discipline to help the company. It's hard to change if you are stuck in the old ways, but it can make all the difference.

I changed my schedule in the service department from going in at 8:30 in the morning to 7. I am doing Facebook Live videos out of the service departments. That takes discipline.

You have to invest in people. Get the training, then turn around and coach others. Go to seminars. Learn. Discipline yourself to learn something new every day. When I'm training someone who doesn't have the discipline to listen or invest in themselves, then sorry, you may be my best friend, but I've got to take my life to another level and you're not coming with me. Either you are with me or against me. But you can't be both. I'm not saying you should fire them right away, but try to get them all the help they need.

People don't get that the universe, or the industry is changing on a daily basis. The economy is changing on a daily basis. I told my employees the other day, why do you upgrade your phone every time there is an upgrade on the phone? You want to get the latest gadgets, the latest updates on apps. Why don't you upgrade yourself? Have you ever thought about it? Everything you learn is upgrading yourself. Upgrade your mindset. People don't want it because it's not comfortable. It's not easy. To upgrade yourself means putting in more hours, both at the office and at home.

One powerful tool in discipline is accountability. People need to check in with each other, personally and in meetings. What did you learn? How did the sale go? I need accountability from everybody. If you are accountable, you get higher productivity and you can accomplish amazing things.

Loyalty

Loyalty is the buzzword for customers. But what about employees? What connection do you have with your workers? Loyal employees are the people who:

- Truly know your work ethic.

- Know your meaning and your core values.

- Know what you stand for.

- Know what you have done for them.

- Know the things that impacted your life.

- Believe in your vision and stick by you.

- Tell you what their future looks like.

- Make sure there is no malice.
- Are not fake.

A loyal employee is a friendship that can last forever. There is a lot of fake people out there. That just want to take a bite out of you, and they want part of your success. They are with you just because of the money. Or because you are buying their lunch when you go out. Some are just loyal to their situation—their moment demands it. Once that stops, the loyalty stops.

Loyalty can create bonds stronger than simple employee and employer relationships. Loyal employees will go through a lot of issues with you, and you know them from behind cameras. I know the real person they are. So when a customer claims my employee did something bad, I can say I don't care what anyone says, I know that person. He would never do something like that.

How do you build loyalty in a person?

- If you hear something they need to know, or you need to give them bad news or train them in a problem area, tell them straight.
- Give them context for everything. Tell them what you are thinking, how what you're saying will help the company, and how it will help them as a person.
- Never talk behind someone's back.
- It's hard for people to stay loyal if they really envy you. Share.
- Respect their opinion about everything, including you.
- If there is anger, talk about it. Don't let it

simmer.

Opinions and Authenticity

Who am I am to judge people? I don't know anything about that person. I don't even know what's going on with their parents or their sister's life. And yet, those people I know nothing about turn around and say things about me because of what they see on social media. I post too much. I must be arrogant. I'm overworking or a workaholic. I had to take stock of what is really happening.

We are judgmental creatures. We judge people for what we see, even just a glance, and that's not reality. Reality is so much more complex than just a quick view into someone's life. If they have opinions of me, that's fine. They've only seen a quick sliver, a tiny fraction of who I am.

Judgments are the brain's feature to tell in an instant whether something is a threat or not, but it's been refined to judge people in relationships, introductions, business, and more. For example, my competitors always talk bad about me because I'm a threat. The tiny bit they know about me is threatening to their business. They want to be like me. But if they knew the real me, we might actually be good friends. Instead, when you are successful, people just want to take a bite out of your apple.

That's why authenticity is so important. To I think open and authentic is to be real. Here I am. Judge away, but I'm not hiding anything from you. And it blew up social media, because I am not a cookie cutter guy. Instead, I'm an honest, open car salesman. I say how I feel. I say it how I see it. And people love that rawness. You are going to get the real deal, and whether you like it or not, you are going to respect my hustle.

There's the alternate side. At the end of the day, if my

employee messes up, I will tell them so. That's on you not on me. Being authentic isn't about boasting you're better than anyone else. Instead, it's about honesty. Be authentic. Be you!

Not many people are authentic enough to share they were in prison, yet here I am. And my journey can help you overcome your problems, too. I am authentic and I will stick to my story. Regardless if someone doesn't want to do business with me because I am an ex-con. I am a convicted felon. I know many ex-cons that are millionaires and have made themselves into something. Authenticity is very important because you never know who needs to hear your story. It says a lot about who you are. Truly who you are. Many people fake it because they want to be someone else. Which is a miserable place to be.

Authentically appreciating your customer comes from the heart. You have to honestly like them, care for them. What does authenticity look like when caring for your customer?

- Listen to them. Again. Listen to your customers. This is vital. If you don't pay attention to the little things, you're going to lose them.

- Follow up. Call, email, text—however they want to stay in contact. Actively look for the product they need.

- Give them what they want. Don't try to fit them into a car or product they don't want.

- Don't say one thing online and then, when the customer gets in the door, tell them another. If the car you feature is $20k, sell it for $20k, not $24k. That would be dishonest.

- Be willing to do whatever it takes to help them.

Be ready to meet their needs.

- Be willing to give free advice. Any life advice they need. Even the self-hurting advice that it's cheaper to repair a car than buy a new one (sometimes).

- Chase the opportunity not the money. The opportunity to help them. To sell them a car. The money takes care of itself.

- I'm willing to educate myself on something the customer needs to know.

- Take chances. Risk doing something that others don't do. Keep a small present ready for every purchase such as movie tickets to enjoy the night out in their new car. Things that are different. Be willing to help and do things that no one else is doing.

Involvement in missions has taught me that I must take care of myself before I can take care of others. That means looking for opportunities so the money will flow in. By thinking big, keeping my goals on the wall where I can see them, I'm able to be self-motivated so I can care for my employees and with their loyalty, and in turn, win the repeated business of customers. By being authentic, I can be myself, enjoy the time I'm working, and create a brand that is talked about all over the world.

My story is one of success. And so is yours. But what's next? What does the future hold for you and me? Let's take a look at how we can maintain this level of success and take it straight to the bank.

WORKBOOK

Chapter Seven Questions

Question: Look at the list of aggressive sales strategies. Which ones are you doing well, and which ones do you need to improve on? How can you work together within your sales team to help each other develop in these areas and to keep up with the evolving market?

_____

_____

_____

_____

_____

_____

_____

_____

_____

_____

Question: What is the vibe that customers get when they come to your establishment?

What is the culture where you work? Are there people who are exhibiting and/or spreading negativity, complacency, or hostility?

If you are in a position of leadership: Who needs to be fired and who needs to be reprimanded, retrained, or encouraged? Which of the motivational tactics do you need to implement? How are you modeling self-discipline and rewarding it in your employees? Where are the loyalties of the current staff and how will you build greater loyalty?

_____

_____

_____

_____

_____

_____

_____

_____

_____

_____

Action: What do you need to put on your "wall"—a check, a photograph, a mission statement? What is your dream and how can you dream it bigger and bolder? Place that motivating visual in a place where you will see it often and where it can help you to stay focused on your overarching goal.

_____

_____

_____

_____

_____

_____

_____

_____

_____

_____

Chapter Seven Notes

CHAPTER EIGHT

The Future

The future is about goals. About making sure you're moving forward, because if you're not progressing, you're moving backward.

My goal is to have my own chain of dealerships, probably in New York. I am going to be running my own show. I am going to have my own auto group. It will be the most powerful social media dealership in the world, dominating every dealer anywhere. I want to make it to the next level. If it works for me, then it works everyone.

When you're progressing forward, it's important not to take things for granted. The key is to be completely self-aware at all times.

I spoke at the same conference as a friend in Vegas. He texted me, "Are you happy? You seem out of sorts? Was I imagining things?"

I am usually in a happy state of mind. I am a happy guy. However, even the most positive people need support every now and then. And in Vegas, I didn't realize I wasn't in the right frame of mind. He said, "I am always here for you." I needed that. I had not been self-aware, and unfortunately, I was letting negativity control me. So, I learned to take charge of my feelings and it has changed my life forever.

Awareness and self-control are such powerful tools. You can control your own feelings. Staying positive in negative situation is always beneficial. I used to go nuts and let people have it when I lost my temper. I used to get fired. Lashing out meant I kept losing. It just isn't worth it. Today it's sunny outside, I am sitting by my pool reading my book, I nothing to complain about, and I take that attitude anywhere I go.

To control your feelings is to control your future. You are able to manage the emotional decisions, and instead make decisions that help your future instead of feeling good in the moment.

By not taking things for granted, you make sure you cover all the possible outcomes of any decision. But truly, things could go bad at any time, and people don't realize what they have until it's gone. You sometimes to forget to thank your Higher Power. God is faithful. He keeps me grounded and keeps me humble. And I don't forget where I come from and who gives me the strength to go on.

Again, like discussed in the last chapter, accountability is valuable I have a circle of four or five people and we're tight. I truly say they are my best friends. They know the real Rudy. Others don't spend enough time with me to know me so deeply. Grow friendships that are this close. They will remind you of your goals, keeping you focused on what you really want, what you really need. If you stray, you'll need a good excuse, and if you don't, it's probably an emotional decision that needs to be stopped. Take the time to build these friendships.

The Secret to Happiness

Every person, from their first to their last breath, are looking for the secret to happiness. There isn't one, and chasing the secret is only going to distract you from the goals that will bring as much happiness as possible. For me, I know fulfillment makes me happier than raw activities that should cause happiness. Happiness is a state of mind, and I am living my dream. I wake up every day and I don't feel like I have a job. I'm doing what I love. The cliché, "Love what you do, and you don't have to work a day in your life" is true. I love going to work. I love doing what I do. I love inspiring people.

But for some, managing car dealerships is a nightmare. They would rather deliver the mail. Or anything else. The secret to happiness comes from inside. It belongs to you and no one else. I can only offer a rough guide to finding it.

Be positive. Putting out the positive image will help you change people's day. It's about impacting that one person. And when you do, the positive vibes from the person will return. It's the law of attraction.

Make time to spend with the ones you love. I spent quality time with my kids, although not as much as I want to. I make it their time. I respect their time. It's a beautiful thing.

Help the core people in your life understand your mission and understands what you are trying to accomplish. Because I have some folks I can hang around and be myself, I can enjoy the moment without worrying about being liked.

Happiness is a state of mind. I may have a bad moment, but I don't live there. Know your purpose, and know you're not inspired to make a living but to make a difference in people's lives. I think that's the most powerful road to happiness. It's not having a million dollars in the bank. I'll never have enough. I know that.

Do more self-improvement instead of criticizing people. Think about personal improvement and less about how other people are troublesome. Work on areas of life that you aren't good at. Because everyone is good at a lot of things. But focusing on your strengths while improving your weaknesses adds value to your life. You might be good at following up with customers. Perhaps you're good at social media. And yet, you may fail with time management. You can play to your strengths and work on your weaknesses. Improve yourself if you aren't good at relationships or connecting with people. Or if you get angry all the time. If you have mixed feelings or panic attacks. These trouble areas offer room for improvement.

I'm going to die with memories, not with dreams. And not just my memories, but other people will remember me. I'm not going to give up. I'm not going to leave the industry the same when I leave, and neither are you. I want people to say, "Hey this guy helped me out. He did what he had to do to change our mentality and change our ways." I think that's why I keep pushing and pushing to be great.

In the first chapter, I talked about using my picture to start a brand. I do the same on social media. Sharing my history will help others find their way to their brand. Share your history with the world and you can be a better person.

People will do one of two things when they see you are excelling in life. They'll be inspired. Or they will be jealous. I think you can inspire people if they truly want to make that switch and are willing to get out of their comfort zone. You won't know about all the lives you'll change, and the key will be to ignore the possibilities and just be yourself. The future will take care of itself.

The future needs you to be on the offense. It needs you to attack it, not be on the defense and wait for events to run you over. A defensive mode is arguing with a person, which makes you just two dumb people arguing over something pointless. Refuse to argue. Attack the problem, not the people. Sometimes I stay quiet. Sometimes remaining silent is more powerful than making a bunch of noise.

At one time, I was the guy making all the noise. The dog that barks but doesn't bite. The alternative, to be on the offensive is to attack, just like the silent dog that snaps without warning. I'm the silent guy now. I bite when I need to, but there's no need to battle constantly with people.

Stop focusing on the little things. Focusing on the paycheck to paycheck will only attract small thinking. Forget about what you are thinking for the future and take it to the next level and be a gamechanger. Crazy money will come in. Expand yourself and open up your horizons to more than one source of income. People will see your skills and ask you to market for them or will desire some other skill you've honed.

If you take these thoughts and create a happier you, the future will take care of itself. Clinging to the care you give yourself will put you in a position to be the best you. And the money will come in.

Chapter Eight Questions

Question: Who are the people who keep you accountable? Do you have an inner circle of friends who know you at a deep level and who have freedom to speak truth into your life whenever it is needed?

_____

_____

_____

_____

_____

_____

_____

_____

_____

_____

_____

Question: What gives you the most lasting happiness? When do you feel most fulfilled and know that you have made a difference? How can you create a happier you by changing your thinking and developing yourself?

_____

_____

_____

_____

_____

_____

_____

_____

_____

_____

Action: What is your story? Write a blog post or make a video to share who you are. Share with authenticity and positivity. Use your story to build relationships with coworkers and customers and to help them find and achieve their goals and dreams.

_____

_____

_____

_____

_____

Chapter Eight Notes

_____

_____

_____

_____

_____

_____

_____

_____

_____

_____

_____

_____

_____

_____

_____

_____

_____

_____

_____

_____

_____

_____

CONCLUSION

Your Turn to Rise

I once had nothing, and now I'm the rising star of the car industry. You can rise, too. There's enough room for all of us to be gamechangers.

A gamechanger plays the game by his or her own rules. They know who they are, and how to move forward with their skills. True, some lessons are learned the hard way along the way, like me going to prison, but if you learn from problems, they can't be called mistakes or failure.

Overcoming the troubles in my past has made me who I am today. And by staying on track, you can use your past experiences to build an empire. You're building to be mentally, physically, and spiritually strong.

Take care of yourself and you'll find yourself in a position to take care of others. Stay positive and humble and keep working hard, and you'll be heading up and speaking at conferences, like me. And by encouraging strong loyalty in both customers and employees, you'll create a fanbase that will keep your business flowing.

Thank you for taking this journey with me. I hope you've been able to learn from my experiences. If you ever walk into one of my dealerships one day, ask for El Patronn. I'd like to meet you and hear how you plan on being a gamechanger.

About the Author

Rudy Treminio was born in El Salvador. His parents did what they had to do to bring their family to America. Rudy started in the automotive business very young and brought himself up through the ranks using his energy, skills, and dedication to process. He built his knowledge on technology and how it impacts business today, becoming a digital warrior who currently serves as acting CEO and president of some of the country's leading technologies.

After turning around six automotive dealerships to be highly successful in markets that were considered difficult, Rudy became managing partner, and he is now turning his success into coaching, conferences, and his Facebook Live show. He earned the handle "El Patronn" in acknowledgement of his leadership over the past fifteen years, with over a half billion dollars in sales and nearly 1.3 million followers. Rudy has no fear and believes that mind over matter, knowledge of your industry, consistent behavior, and building a positive culture with your team will reward every business with real success.

About Speak It To Book

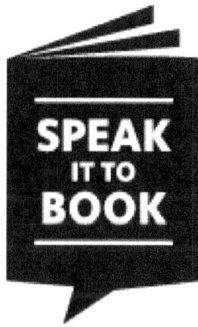

Speak It to Book is revolutionizing how books are created and used.

Traditional publishing requires thousands of hours, and then you're asked to surrender your rights. Self-publishing is indicative of a poor-quality product with no prestige. And neither model boasts results-driven marketing.

That's why we created a better option. Speak It To Book has the attention of the industry because we are disrupting it in a brilliant way.

Imagine:

- What if you had a way to get those ideas out of

your head?

- What if you could get your story in front of the people who need it most?
- What if you took the next step into significance and influence?

You can accomplish all of these goals by writing a book. Plus, you can do it without having to use a pencil, and in less than one-tenth of the time!

Your ideas are meant for a wider audience. So step into significance—by speaking your story into a book.

Visit www.speakittobook.com to learn more.

REFERENCES

Notes

---

[1] Cardone, Grant. *The 10x Rule.* Wiley, 2011.

www.ingramcontent.com/pod-product-compliance
Lightning Source LLC
LaVergne TN
LVHW051417080426
835508LV00022B/3122